Sumac's Red Arms

Sumac's Red Arms

Karen Shklanka

For Laura,
I hope you enjoy it!

COTEAU BOOKS

Edited by Liz Philips
Cover design by Duncan Campbell
Book design by J. Lauder Publishing & Design

Cover image: "Woman's Feet Moving on Dance Floor" by Corbis Photography/Veer Inc.

Printed and bound in Canada at Gauvin Press

The inside pages of this book are printed on recycled paper containing 100% post-consumer fiber.

Mixed Sources
Product group from well-managed forests and recycled wood or fiber
www.fsc.org Cert no. SGS-COC-2624
© 1996 Forest Stewardship Council
FSC

Library and Archives Canada Cataloguing in Publication

Shklanka, Karen, 1963-
    Sumac's Red Arms / Karen Shklanka

Poems.
ISBN 978-1-55050-402-6

I. Title.
PS8637.H527S94 2009   C811'.6   C2009-901030-5

10 9 8 7 6 5 4 3 2 1

COTEAU BOOKS

2517 Victoria Ave.
Regina, Saskatchewan
Canada   S4P 0T2

Available in Canada and the US from:
Fitzhenry & Whiteside
195 Allstate Parkway
Markham, Ontario
Canada L3R 4T8

The publisher gratefully acknowledges the financial assistance of the Saskatchewan Arts Board, the Canada Council for the Arts, the Government of Canada through the Book Publishing Industry Development Program (BPIDP), the Association for the Export of Canadian Books, the Cultural Industries Development Fund of Saskatchewan and the City of Regina Arts Commission for its publishing program.

Canada Council for the Arts   Conseil des Arts du Canada

SASKATCHEWAN ARTS BOARD

Canada

Regina
CITY OF REGINA
Regina Arts Commission

in memory of Elizabeth Marion Cameron,
my grandmother

and for Eric

Table of Contents

The Only Living Things

The Scent of Cloves

Vocabulary: A Tango

Cradle

The Under wings of Clouds

The Only Living Things

Whom can I ask what I came
to make happen in this world?

Pablo Neruda, *The Book of Questions*

Moose Factory, Ontario

JULY 1

It's Canada Day, somewhere between blackflies
and mosquitos, nobody out but a few Cree children,
when I'm called from home to stitch up James
who woke bleeding on a battlefield of empties
and limp friends. He walked to the hospital
though he didn't feel any pain yet.
Blood-clotted hair holds edges of scalp;
I feel his skull through the wound.
He doesn't want me to shave his head.
I use 2-0 Nylon to suture, take big bites
with my curved needle.

My beeper whines. It's not Ward 2
needing Tylenol for Mrs. Kataquapit's arthritis,
it is an outside call, my friend Matthew,
says he's been sitting all morning with a gun to his head.
Last time I picked him up by snowmobile.
Today he offers to walk to my house.

When he arrives, silk shirt wrinkled from the night before,
I think he is the most beautiful man I've ever seen,
though one of his front teeth is cracked and black
so he smiles with his mouth closed.
My eager Husky jumps to greet him.
I want to take his shiny hair in my hands
but I am his wife's doctor.
His brown eyes look right through me.
We hug, hips held back a little.
I make tea.

Feet up on the railing, he sits on my porch
watching elders stroll the dusty road.
In his soft Cree accent, Matthew tells me stories
of his grandfather's dog sled postal service,
then he speaks of the pot, the hash, the coke.
He says booze isn't a problem.
He got fired, sold his CDs, stole from Mom,
his wife had an affair, grandfather died of cancer.
Then his best friend left a party, broke through the river ice
on a snowmobile, and died.
Shadows lengthen on the hospital road.
We walk to the schoolyard full of squealing kids,
feathers, balloons, drumming.
My beeper pinches, I run home, dial the hospital.
Switchboard transfers me to emergency-
James is back, feeling the pain now, shaking.
I hesitate before going in. The nurse laughs.
She says, "The liquor store's closed.
A six pack of Valium'll take care of his pain
until Monday." I grab my stethoscope and supper,
Canada Day bannock from the fridge.
The twenty dollar bill on my kitchen counter
has disappeared.

On my walk to the hospital, laughter
drifts from schoolyard celebrations.
A white balloon blows down the empty street.

OCTOBER 2

In orange and turquoise Gore-Tex, duck boots,
I am ready for the goose hunt. Donald laughs
just as he does when I try to speak Cree. He finds me
hip-waders and khaki, the colours of his life.
On water, cold is colder. It takes an hour to cross the river
winding toward the salt of the bay that has no shore,
only muskeg sinking into sea.
Don jumps from the freighter canoe,
pulls until it scrapes on the mucky bottom.
He smiles, points with his chin, and I follow.
We crouch in the grass. He calls the geese
before I see the small vee.

      Mike grew up here, hunted this delta. I cannot call him
      now, wrap my arms around my thighs, curl into memory.
      I tasted that sweet alcohol
      on his breath when he came back
      from wherever he went for days.
      An apology of red carnations
      grew from green styrofoam on my doorstep.
      When he came back. If.
      I looked down at my hands,
      kneading bread we would eat.
      Through my window, sky wide as wings,
      stunted spires of trees dark across the river.
      A deer, all legs, leaned to its reflection in the water,
      startled at my call, ran.

The geese come to Don, return his call. Two shots,
the honking veers. There are two birds limp in the shallows.
He retrieves them, holds them by those thick necks,
puts one warm and heavy into my hands.
The river flows silently. A marshland quiet surrounds us.
Now it seems we are the only living things.

DECEMBER 13

The ambulance drives up to the front door
of the hospital, with a man who'd left one of those
all-night Moose Factory parties, went home
and hung himself. His suspicious
girlfriend followed him, cut him
down before he stopped breathing.
The attendants bring him into the ER
unconscious. It's 0300 hours.
You always feel cold at that time of night
in a hospital. I am the only doctor here.
I've never seen marks on a neck like that,
a face that colour.

MARCH 24

That afternoon at the hospital
I open the door to the morgue, see Will
with his hands in the black hair of his best friend.
Blood washes into the sink.
Metal tray, white plastic sheet,
a silver faucet's tall curve,
Daniel's pale feet, still.

I think of an all-night party,
an icy Sunday morning, a fast Skidoo,
how Will wasn't on the ambulance,
would have slept it off if he hadn't had the call.
When Daniel hit the snow, his heart
swung open on the great arch of the aorta,
the tide of blood receding from the brain.

Death is the seep of salt water
into soil, sea grass, muskeg, ice,
a caught-in-the-throat sound
that falls through air light with geese.

The Girl From Attawapiskat

She is the fifth Friday night "Tylenol overdose" sent from the Attawapiskat nurses in six weeks. I am new to medicine, to the North, still can't sleep nights before being on-call. We chopper them down: fifteen or sixteen years old, smooth skin, wary eyes. I never really know what to do. There's no acetaminophen level. No proof. They get an IV drip for the night, Mucomyst, then go shopping at the Northern store the next day. There's not much for a teenager to do in Attawapiskat, a reserve of a thousand people with their own Cree dialect. Once, we made the rule, "No Shopping," and the weekend helicopter rides stopped, for a while.

Another Saturday night, the girl from Attawapiskat again. An "overdose." She refuses to stand, so I sit on the floor of the ER with her. Her voice is quiet, not wanting to talk to me. She casts her eyes down. I wait. Look at the scuffmarks on the floor.

She says she heard a voice in her head that gave orders. Kill yourself, the voice says. This time, I know what to do. There is a psychiatric hospital in North Bay. The psychiatrist can't refuse. The pilots flying patients to this hospital insist they wear a straightjacket. We both cry as the orderlies strap her in. She screams at the men. I stand in the stairwell by the helicopter pad. She spits on me as they wheel her out on the stretcher.

Four months later the girl from Attawapiskat stops me on the road, as I walk to the hospital. I hardly recognize her. She is pretty now. A bit plumper. From the medication, I think. Not as quiet. Says she wants to thank me for sending her to North Bay, that she'd been in treatment for depression, sexual abuse. She appreciates me taking the time. Plans to go and stay with her older sister in Fort Albany. I blush, then release my breath; fight the tears in my eyes.

♀♀

Six months later I get a call at 10 pm from the nurse in Fort Albany, one community north from Moose Factory on James Bay. A thirty-five year old woman has been in a gas explosion. From medical school, I know the key question is, *Does she have burns around her mouth? Yes? Then check inside. Yes? Bits of black?* My mind is tight and clear.

I send the anesthetist up in the chopper in case of swelling of her airway, then I fall asleep on the living room floor, a blanket over my shoulders, my husband in the bedroom upstairs. The phone wakes me up at midnight. I've been drooling. Don't know where I am. The nurse is panicking. The chopper isn't there yet. The patient is choking.

I talk the nurse through a needle cricothyroidotomy. It doesn't work. *There's blood everywhere,* she says. *Get the bag and mask, oxygen,* I say, *some air will get in.* They hear the chopper. Hang up.

I can't sleep, call an hour later to see what's happened. She was barely hanging in there when the doctor arrived, then she lost her IV. I'd asked for two, but they'd only managed one, her veins were so shut down. While they all tried to replace the IV, she stopped breathing, had a cardiac arrest. The nurse says the woman's sister, the girl from Attawapiskat, is waiting outside.

First Pregnancy

Her secret pockets of fear cannot
be measured, unlike blood pressure,
urine sediments, the height
of an egg-shaped uterine body
above the pubic symphysis,
the fetal heart rate.

Trained merely to name, I murmur
Downs, Klinefelter's, Fetal Alcohol
Syndrome, Crie-de-Chat.
Small faces with short upper lips,
ears a bit low, a narrow smile,
limbs that don't bounce back.

Trimester to trimester to trimester, I follow
with medical books, triple test results
ultrasound photographs,
gravid with expectations -
beat of heart, wave of fetal arm.
We want perfection in the genome.

The mother's carrying high, hips widening.
How to recognize labour
in all the squeezings and pullings?
Weekly, I judge blood pressure,
swollen feet, sugar or protein
spilling in her urine.

After all the tests are fine
comes the hardest one of all.
The father is a pale satellite,
the mother is on a different planet.
My nurse and I follow dilatation, descent,
fetal heart rate's ups and downs.
Press of scalp hard on the perineum,
I push back against the labia's
impossible shout and thrust.
The head appears.
The woman looks at me
in the space between legs and belly

the baby down too low now
for the Doppler to hear.
I guide her hand to the wet black hair,
and we wait for the after-coming shoulder.
There is a gush of fluid and slippery limbs.
I catch the slick body, warm in my gloved hands.

Moose Factory, the North, Good Sex

To keep myself comfortable, I used to insist
that he and I take turns, each at our own end
with our own little thing to do.
The one-person-at-a-time approach to sex,
kind of like playing hockey or broomball
and you're the one with the puck.
There was a goal. I always got there.

For years after I left Moose Factory
and the North, good sex made me cry.
You know, the sensation where you lose
the edges of your own body.
It's like skating on a frozen river,
you feel you can go on and on
forever.

The Scent of Cloves

We shall not cease from exploration
And the end of all our exploring
Will be to arrive where we started
And know the place for the first time.

T.S. ELIOT

The Scent of Cloves

I savour the noisy market, the slow
hiss of clams, the cool breath of oysters, secrets
from the mussel's orange tongue. The air
is heavy with the scent of cloves, black tea.
My fingers stream through aniseed and cardamom.
Richard Burton walks with me
in the Old Town. We explore
the Mountains of the Moon
to find the source of the Nile.
We march long days
under the Sultan's red flag. We play
black and white games with Colubus monkeys.
The wild boars startle, lift their tails and run away.

He speaks to me in Eastern words
of tantric sex. We sleep in the heat
of the afternoon. He posts watch
for crocodiles. I splash in the river
then take clean linen from a Zanzibar
chest to dress for dinner.

We end each safari with his voice, his stories
touching the shell of my ear. I taste
the flesh of a gazelle, brandy
on his tongue.

A Certain Yellow

My mother peels a golden persimmon,
then slices it into a bowl.
I think of a happier Van Gogh. His yellow.
How he filled the house at Arles,
sunflower paintings to welcome Gauguin.

When I visit my mother
she serves fruit for me every day,
small, pale mangoes from Mexico,
strawberries, blueberries, whatever are in season.
She slices oranges and grapefruits,
tosses them with pomegranate seeds.

Once we stayed at a hacienda in Oaxaca,
sat under a pomegranate tree in the courtyard
in the morning. They served hot chocolate,
pinwheels of papaya, watermelon, mango,
and fruit we couldn't name in English.

At home I take my morning orange,
my mother's knife, carve through
the pith, follow the fruit's curves.
I drop the sections into a striped bowl,
leave the membranes, squeeze them for juice,
sprinkle sun dried cranberries on top.

Whenever I see a certain yellow
in a Gauguin painting, I know
he was thinking of Van Gogh.
A persimmon has large seeds, slippery flesh.
I feel its weight in my hand.

Chastising the Rhinoceros

The hill's large darkness
circles the house, arbutus branches
stretch across the yard. Night air
sinks humid and cool to the ground.

A rhinoceros stands
in the short green grass, incongruous
as the Self. A woman in bra and panties, high heels,
chatters at the animal, waves her finger.

Stubby legged, it tastes
azalea leaves, nibbles around twisted red limbs
at the arbutus trunk, the awkward horn
tearing strips of bark.

The woman takes a step back
toward the house. The rhino stops,
waits. Light from the doorway
illuminates its face.

Punta Indio

Thirty-four degrees
in the shade, even the monkeys
are quiet.

Iguanas silver the roof tiles.
Palm trees whisper
across the dry valley: sleepy
bedroom voices.

Our bodies swell
with summer.

My pregnant sister, breasts
large under black Lycra,
follows her round belly
into the pool.

That lilt in her voice
tells me she's listening.
The season is endless,

here, our hands sticky
with mangoes
and lime juice.

I return to my hammock, while she settles
in deep water.

Tempting a Diabetic

for Yvonne

The mysterious fruit in a Frida Kahlo painting at the La Palacio des Bellas Artes in Mexico City is called *tuna*. It comes from the prickly pear cactus, and must be picked with care. A luminous magenta. The prickly pear has the sharpest spines in the world: approaching the cactus paddles is a risky venture. I've tried it. The plant reminds me of you, not because you are spiny – whether that means multiple dangerous-to-touch units for photosynthesis or a decisive stack of vertebrae – but because the fruit regulates blood sugar. I want to take away the little machine you stab at your fingertips, feed you *tuna* sorbet, *tuna* cheesecake, *tuna* marmalade on poached pears with red wine, a culinary tango. I'll come to Norwich, bring you cactus-infused olive oil to rub into your hands.

Hands and Stories

Dad locks us out by mistake.
You pull the pins out of the *palapa* door,
take it off its hinges.

We go inside and make guacamole,
black beans, salad with these strange fruits.
You don't know a papaya

is a yellow football full of seeds
like round black beads.

Your painful Spanish tells Santo the night watchman,
Working at night is good birth-control.
I know he gets it by his laugh.

Another story stalled when you couldn't find
the word for shit in the dictionary.
We play motorboat in the pool.

We see a red and black slithering in the bush,
so Georgia rides on your shoulders. Dad says, *I forgot
to tell you there are 17 species of poisonous snakes.*

Every rustle is no longer an iguana.
Purple and orange crabs fall out of the drainpipes.

El Viejo

Off Las Ramblas, the Barcelona street,
I pass Indian restaurants, garbage piled outside.
An old man takes his cat for a ride
in a yellow crate with wheels. When we meet
halfway down a four-bakery block where sweet
cream-filled pastries tempt me inside,
I am close enough to smell his scent, see the pride
in his antique jacket, neatly pressed shirt and pants.

It's his tie that fascinates, brown, dark
wool with scattered sequins fuscia-pink,
each circled with a black pen mark.
He returns my stumbling Spanish, ink-
black fingers waving the words apart.
I smile. He winks.

Waiting

The woman is in Seville without
her husband; is learning to move her lips
in the vowels of a new language. Wings
of *palomas* sweep the early morning
plaza; she hears throaty *coo-coos*
from the lintel, where the doves
land just above her head. Winter
jasmine locks up its nighttime
scent. The dark city is already
crowded with commuters. When
she steps off the bus, an elderly woman
in black speaks to her in Spanish
so fast, she can't keep up. Last
night, her heels echoed
along the streets as she lost
herself in the Jewish quarter
after the class party. Today she hums
in time to her strides, thinks of herself
as the flamenco dancer in the Spanish
grammar book. The dancer beats
her feet on the ground; her hands
curl upward like smoke from
burning leaves on a still day.
The sun rises above the low
apartment buildings. For
a moment, streets are on fire, orange
trees flame with morning. The waiter
sweeping leaves into the plaza
is short and dark. She smells coffee
as a customer opens the door
to leave the cafe. She steps
inside and sits down, glances
at her pale hands on the table.

The Morning Offers Itself

Fog drapes the salt grass
on the flats. Despite the cool breeze, sweat
beads between my breasts,
along my spine.

A white ibis stands
on the rocks, sentinel,
just beyond the wharf. She bows
her curved beak to the water,

while a turtle lies
on half-submerged dock.
A 'peacock' hops from Texas pine to rooftop –
his call rakes the air. How is he confined?

A great egret fishes
the shore, snaps up
prey with the suddenness
of more long-winged birds.

The day is a message
in a blue bottle;
from the rocks nearby, an oyster
breathes the sea.

Solo

"Being alone in an airplane for even so short a time as a night and a day can be as startling as the first awareness of a stranger walking by your side at night. You are the stranger."

- Beryl Markham

It took two years for Beryl to forget her
mother's face, after she left for England,
but she remembered her scolding
while she brushed Beryl's tangled
blonde hair. Her strokes hurt, but
the little girl never cried.

One time Beryl ran from Equator Ranch
with a new spear, into the Kenyan jungle.
Under a juniper tree, she came face
to face with a lion whose yellow eyes
stopped her. She sang the marching song
of the King's African Rifles; turned
to walk away. Bishon Singh, a servant,
saw the half-tame lion pass, then
the girl. He ran after Beryl. "A lion
and a girl: not good company!"
The lion jumped on her back. The gashes
on Beryl's skin healed in twelve days.
The lion was caged for life.

December is hot in Kenya. No draft stirs
the Christmas angels on the tree. Beryl learns
to hunt with a bow and arrow, afraid
of nothing, except losing her father,
or his respect. A new governess
moves in. Beryl hides a dead snake
in her bed, argues, "A gown and halo
are silly things to fly in." She nails
branches together, layers them with wings
of guinea fowl, jumps off the roof
of the barn. Skinny long legs
in khaki, the only girl who runs
with the Kipsigis boys, she imagines
her mother dead of malaria, not
a silence in her father's mouth.

The Anguish of Women

You mustn't always believe what I say.

- Pablo Picasso

Side by side, looking away
from each other, these are two
of Picasso's women, painted the same
year. Both his lovers. One the mother
of his child. They could be
my sister and I, resting against
the wall at the Musée Picasso
in Paris, taking a break, observing
the passersby. This one, a woman who
doesn't realize what she knows. Arms
draped over the back of the chair, all
the hues of a fading bruise in her bias-cut
dress, she is patient with Picasso,
his criticism, his other lives. That one,
the Weeping Woman, her nails like
daggers, her intelligence sheathed, still
knows too much. Men give her
everything but what she desires. All
her colours cry – me, me, me-
to a world without ears. From month
to month, year to year, Picasso measures
their necessities as if the answer
is a number; his cheque always
in the mail. Once committed
to canvas, he can leave them
without needs, at rest, gazing outward.

From the gallery wall, Dora, with the red eye, grabs
museum visitors by the arm, says, Listen – *let me
tell you – he was a Minotaur*, and takes their
photograph. Marie-Therese, the blonde
goddess, doesn't reach out.

When you see the two of them together
on the wall, you wouldn't know that a few
days later, their patina crumbled, they wrestled
each other, tried to force Picasso to choose
between them.

The Painter and Time

The water mark on her ceiling expands,
cold egg bonds with the cast-iron fry pan,

wind squeals between wall-boards,
the kitchen floor is furred with catkins.

This in-between time, lives are being spliced.
She paints being a wife, somewhere between breakfast,

her parents' appointments with the doctor,
return of the school bus, replacement

of a party dress in the dress-up box.
The roofer is on his way.

A discarded piece of wood, a paintbrush:
she outlines a woman in a narrow black dress, who reaches

out of the picture. She bends down on the stairs.
Her high heels are like the tall-awkward feet

of a deer walking up the deck
to taste the azalea on the top step. She is heedless.

The woman in the picture sneaks in the back door.
In the artist's kitchen, there are stacks of paper. A watermark.

Something you can only see
in certain light.

Vocabulary : A Tango

. . . pleasure – taken to its extremity – becomes work.
And work – taken to its extremity – becomes love.

- Sally Potter, director of *The Tango Lesson*

Vocabulary: A Tango

1. abrazo

her look, an invitation.

in the circle of
          his arms
she lets go of knowing

2. vals

the lead.
      the beat.

always her breath
         close to his ear.

she moves
      between notes.

3. *caminata*

he looks ahead
           to where they are going,

touches
his temple
      to hers.

she sees where they've come from
                    closes her eyes

4. *ochos*

lines of their bodies
           just intersect

they explore
       right and left
shoulder and hip
       pivot and step

a moment,
   air,
      a continent

5. volcada

he unbalances her.

she says

toe
of my shoe.

fingers
of my left hand.

little hairs
on your neck
above your collar.

6. gancho

she wraps his thigh
        with her leg –

                        a hook,

            an un-
                hinging

7. molinete

she says –

    I walk around
you,   you're   always
in the centre.

let's change places.

8. sacada

step forward
between my legs
he asks,
as he moves away from her

then he steps into her space
as she leaves.

they keep doing this.

9. *parada*

she stops him

slides her toe up
and down
his leg,

what I want:
this,
        and this

10. *salida*

together
they pivot away

from each other,

face
            in the same
direction.

his hand
on the side of her chest
just below her breast

11. cruz

he rushes the beat,

                opens

a space

        between her legs,

        closes

            his chest,

to place her away

                from him

           into

        the cross

  (her one thigh

  in front

of the other)

she leans into

her heels

        she un-

           winds.

12. el sanguchito

now.
    she says,
(foot
     toe
foot)
     now.
you've
     got me.

13. colgada

centripetal acceleration, her body

                       leaves him, the
point
    where their feet touch ground, this
                           place
of suspension

14. *voleo*

how her body reacts to him
              when she doesn't
expect it:

     loose, flying

her spiked heels
              deadly

15. *cambio de frente*

he puts his foot down

his momentum translates
into
    (swirling
skirts)
     she
continues

(on)

Cradle

Memento mori, memento vivena.

Death Certificate

Sue needs morphine injections every four hours. Her daughters learn how to put the small needle under her skin, and when she's conscious she never complains. In my office we don't talk much about breast cancer. She always laughs at herself, flatters me. That is her way: charming, bigger than the room. All smiles, widely spaced blue eyes, long grey hair in a braid, wrists exposed below the arms of her grey sweater, green boots rubbing together as she strides down the hall leaving clumps of dirt on the floor, cheeks rosy with alcohol or the outdoors. Both probably. She would be the first to say that. She has a farm. A lovely girlfriend. Lots of family.

The call comes on a Sunday morning when I am being treated to pancakes with maple syrup. I put on silver earrings, drape a stethoscope around my neck, and let Sheeshu into the back of the car. Sue always ruffled her fur at the office. And I don't want to be alone. I swing by the hospital to pick up the death certificate, fill it out, and put it on the passenger seat. A cold December morning, my wheels crack puddle ice as the car crawls around the corner. A llama looks up as I pass. A barn leans to the road, cars sprawl in the driveway, a little dog whines at the door.

I let myself in, enter the room where Sue lies on a hospital bed in the living room, facing windows which frame untended fields, Trincomali Channel, Galiano Island in the distance. Everyone looks at me. For comfort, there is only my ritual. I sit by her on the bed, take her hand, still warm. No pulse. I put my cold stethoscope on her chest without apology. Her muscles have given way to ribs. I hear nothing but my earrings jangling against the metal earpieces. No beat. No air. Her mouth is slightly open.

I can't remember what I say next. My impressions of Sue, perhaps. I take her daughter's hands. Then I drive slowly home. I let Sheeshu out of the car, and she bounds up the driveway to the door. When I let her in, she runs straight to the kitchen to beg for the leftover pancakes.

Portal

Portals of stainless steel,
shrouds for thirty men and women.
Four students per cadaver,
each body with a canvas hood,
each student with a set of tools
in a black plastic case.

Three men and I open
the great steel petals.
We bow over our work,
chant under breath –
maxilla – mandible – zygomatic bone –
symphysis pubis – acetabulum –
obturator canal –

The body drawn
in class, its anatomical
pits, grooves, triangles;
sinuses, foramena and fissures;.
The body mapped red and blue
for arteries and veins,
green for nerves.

This room, chill.
Phenol, the incense
that seeps into our hair,
lingers. We breathe through
our mouths. No questions.
Simple as precise line
of knife, tissue plane.

Only much later do I learn
the way living skin
pulls away from the scalpel.

Aide-Mémoire for a Medical Student: The Hidden Lives of Bones

the first cervical vertebra:

it twirls, hangs
around:

hangman's fracture, ropes
(of pearls)

the radius
and ulna,

they break together
or not at all

transfigure –
oh beautiful clavicle, oh
easily broken
one, darling

how easily you repair
yourself

incus, malleus, stapes

secret place under the
fall of words, wet
kisses behind
(your ear), the (carotid)
pulse of

hear hear!

the left wing of the ileum
flies low.

yes, Georgia, yes. how
it captures the desert
sky!

os sacrum

cradle of Fallopian
tubes,

arrow: direction
underworld

sitting in
meditation

La Cumparsita

By the time her husband stomped off
the dance floor, half-way through the song,
she was thin, with sorry hands.
Their dogs never got along.
She'd started to flinch
when he raised his voice.
There was the condom he put in her wallet
as a going away gift; the birthday dinner
he made to entice her home, uneaten.
She wrote him a post-card
from Seville, said she had fallen in love
with the city of flamenco.
She was really saying:
Now I can dance alone.

Change, A Spiral

Two turkey vultures spiral
through dense trees, swoop
and settle, in a cracking of twigs,
on a big branch in the forest
outside my bedroom window.
One at a time, they drift down
to the base of the hill.
A red head picks at the dead fawn
stretched out on an outcrop of rock,
head flung back, framed by soft ears,
an even row of teeth in the delicate lower jaw,
legs a darker brown, small hoofs
curled under its chin.

How They Divide

She takes the blue Ukrainian teapot,
all the wedding gifts from her side of the family,
leaves him toaster, microwave,
electric coffee maker, second-hand couch.

She keeps the empty wooden chest, antique,
from Belleville; buys a crochet hook and some wool.

He keeps the antique table without any chairs,
eats dinners at the Chinese restaurant.

He takes the Nepalese saddle rug
backpacked from Muktinath
when they couldn't make it over the Pass.

She keeps the prayer wheel
they bought on the road to Pokhara,
which was pitted with meteor holes
and mating dogs.

He takes the antique *kilim* from Cappodochia
where they walked through underground cities,
imagined escaping Alexander the Great.

She keeps the photos of Troy, all nine cities
separated by red petals of poppies, saves them
between pages of the Iliad,

which she puts on her IKEA bookshelf, the one
they bought after graduation, to hold everything
they'd learned up until that point.

Can We Say What's Lost?

When I hold you, there's a hardness
where your right breast used to be.
It's only temporary:
this plastic bag
filled with saline, stretched
under your pectoral muscle;
our hug; life itself.
Next, your breast replaced
with silicone, a nipple
fashioned from the inner thigh's
darker skin, nerves sacrificed
along with pleasure.
They'll make the right breast
smaller, to match the left more closely.
These details matter.

The Body Forgets

Try to regain something long lost:
balance, for fouetté turns across the studio;

stick-to-it-ive-ness, for running arpeggios
up and down the piano after school;
a giddy, twirling glee at the first snow of the season.

Put the pads of the crutches beside your chest,
press them into your sides like wings.

There's a stair, for each time
you replayed the accident in your mind.
Slide down one stair at a time on your bottom.

Celebrate the repetition of healing, press and pull
of the therapist's hands into painful places,

wasting of flesh, roll and lift of limbs,
the movement broken into new components.

The body forgets something this simple.
Patience moves you forward, walks you
into the next stanza.

Retreat

I've left husband and patients to go on retreat.
Outside the farmhouse, geese line up their white

wing stripes between apple trees, peck at the
ground. An eagle on a branch by the water

separates eye from bone – claw to beak – flies
away, a fish dangling from its talons.

My door shudders closed behind me. I'm alone
in the bedroom with a moth, its soft, erratic flight.

Dance When the Fiddle Stops

She said "pirouette"
to her granddaughter
with the curly hair,
who took ballet lessons
at the United Church hall.
She slept with her mouth open
in the afternoon, always
a clean tissue peeking
from her sleeve,
shoulders drooped
with age or years
of teaching high school.
Once she sewed a wedding dress,
smocked, buttonholed by hand,
now her needle follows the curves
of a brown-haired doll.
She clears her blue hairs
from the sink, scatters
rose petals between her slips
in the drawer, saves scraps of lace
and tulle for the ballerina girl,
walks five miles a day
with a bad heart. At this age, goodbyes
are as frequent as going to church
on Sunday. Her husband
was dead at forty-seven.
She saves his fiddle
for her grandson.

Season

Milkweed pods empty themselves to the wind,
dry cups like grandmother's hands.
A child on the bank follows a yellow leaf underwater.
Sumac's red arms gather in the weather.
The river, larger in memory,
pours itself like clear tea through the ravine.

The Dry Tears of a Man

For years you misplaced your wedding
anniversary, Joan said. She was prone
to forgiveness. You asked her to dance
evenings, placed your right hand
across her back, pulled her in close.

Then one day you forgot
to feed the dog, were trying to console
him at dinner-time; forgot
it was spring and the rhododendrons
were out. You,
such a gardener,
accused Joan.

Memory creeps away like the night paws of dogs.
Hindemith still sings from the piano; minor chords
whisper the times you cried
the dry tears of a man.
The time James' dog starved
after he went to Normandy:
she would only eat from his hand.
You remember the dog's eyes.

Time clips thorns; you forget your widowed mother
disowned you, her only son, for marrying
out of the faith. Memories scuttle around
like mice in the crawl space. You forget
you never liked spicy food.
Joan enjoys cooking again.

Irises open their mouths, blow kisses
each morning Joan walks you back
from the end of the driveway
where you wait for your ride to work.

Exploration

I am blindfolded, feel
the Los Angeles sun on my cheeks,
smell jasmine, tomatillos and cornmeal.
I hear horns honking in the distance,
fragments of Spanish from the street.
A faint stench of old urine
wafts from the parkade.
Gemmon leads me,
with her arm around my waist.
We walk side-by-side
through the Japanese garden. She tells me
there are jacaranda blossoms
on the path. I feel her bend
to pick one up
and I bend with her.

After our walk, we gather with the other caregivers.
Half of the group of doctors and nurses
take off our blindfolds; have found a way
to move forward in the dark;
half of us take our hands away
from elbows and waists,
give up responsibility
for the other's steps.

Dear God,

I want to believe you'll get this letter.
It's been on and off between us.
You show up in snowflakes, eyelashes, blackberry pie,
a newborn warm in my hands.

But I've seen too many thick-necked blue bodies,
a tube down the throat. There was the retired history professor,
a kind man, forgetful. He walked down the hall
as I wrote my notes at the nursing station, called to show me
he was up on his feet, and then he collapsed.
On my knees, on the vinyl tiles,
I blew into his mouth, pressed on his chest.
I gave him all the right drugs, felt the warmth leave him.
The cardiogram said bleep, bleep, bleep,
as I held his head in my hands.

Then last winter I met an angel in Berlin.
I sat with her on her stone column.
We looked over the city, the snow, the leafless gardens,
the traffic going around in circles.
Even when I spoke, she didn't look away from them.
I asked to go into the lives of the people,
without sadness and without hope.

Letter to Jesús

You tell me *te extraño mucho*
in your email, and I look up
the words, unsure if you miss me,
or think I'm strange. I don't know
your sense of humour, only your hands
on my back, those days in your dance class
at Banff. We all stood with our legs on the barre,
three writers, Sarah, Lesley, and I
and a family from Mexico with their two kids.
I was at the end of the line.
You went from one to the next
with your soft voice, definitive hands,
straightened the mother's leg, firmly
pressed Sarah's lovely curve
as you did every day, said *stomatch*.
We all tried harder for you, even the boy,
sweat coming out on our upper lips.
We had sore legs all the first week.
When you came to me, you paused
until I looked at you, smiled,
took the strand of hair
that had fallen over my eyes,
tucked it behind my ear.

Today it snowed
in Banff, there were no deer
in the forest, and I could hear the sound
of a tuba through the trees. I thought
of you, how you danced in the studio
with your suitcase, opened
its zippers, investigated its interior
spaces, used it as a door
into memory: you unpacked
a boy, a sad clown, the entire
Mexican circus of your life,
your wish to be different
than you are.

Your studio is empty now,
with a group of composers next door
writing an opera. I walk across
the oak floor to the barre, rock
my weight back on my heels
then raise myself onto my toes
feeling a stretch through the arches
of my feet. I extend until it almost
hurts, until – you might
have said – the small bones
in my feet call out.

Readiness

A month before your birth a wave
breaks on the Bay of Chaleur. I jump
over the wave, run from sandbar
to sandbar; salt-encrusted hairs
stick to my forearms; warm
water splashes above my knees.
A purple jellyfish lies
like a placenta on
the beach. I imagine
it pulsing in
the warm bay.

The Invisible Buddha

There is no knowing how many souls have been formed by this simple exercise.

- John Updike, from *Hoeing*

Bow at the door
        to the empty room.

As you enter,
hold your left hand
below your breastbone,
thumb tucked in.

Cup your right hand
over your left.

Arrive at your place.

Bow to your cushion
and the invisible Buddha.

Turn.

Out the window,
a yellow bloom of iris.

Bow, again,
to your children
who have lent you this earth,
and sit.

The Under wings of Clouds

Vitality shows in not only the ability to persist
but also the ability to start over.

- F. Scott Fitzgerald

My Only Real Virginity

You take my fingers
in your mouth, hello and
hello and hello. I remember
your tongue from a dream
that I was a sheaf of green
onions,
       and then lilies
against the white side of a house.
And,
      a woman again, I flew
down and plucked that spray,
entered through a window, held
the greens against my dress,
a mist of white.

No Apology

We stand on the beach
at Metchosin. In the waves, stones
roll over stones, a fine clatter.
The gulls brace themselves,
rustle their feathers
against the wind. At the edge
of the forest, I watch chickadees
lead the winter forage
from tree to tree, whistle
when they find a new place.
A spotted towhee rummages
in the dry leaves, pauses
to look around with its brilliant red eyes.
I want you to understand
that it hurts me, what you don't know
about yourself, that missing bird;
the one whose call you hear
high in the tree; the one you can't see
though you take your binoculars
everywhere.

Chorus

Frogs thrum the hours. A deer awakens
the dog and me, as – in tense dark air – night
horizons hum between ponds, time
zones, evening news, morning mail;

twisted sheets, bursts of mind jazz, the war
in Iraq, SARS in my brother's city, you,
a pulse, an absence beneath my ribs;

sweat between my breasts and thighs, slippery
trails, dreams fever my brain, sirens
rise and fall on windy Salt Spring roads. A call
from the hospital, my patients narcotic
in demented, dangerous wards.

The dog jumps onto the bed, licks
salt from my face, paws my arm.
She throws back her head, black
lips form an *Ohh*.

You and the deer slip away. Finally,
my patients sleep. I hear the whine
of a morning float-plane,
see the beaded pink lip of dawn.

Untouchable

Half-illuminated, I am the moon: here
is my dark side, here my light. A jealous
angel, I look at you through narrowed eyes.
Slip-slide, I am in your hands, moon
face, barbed silver, tide. Caress
my hair. Hold me against yourself just
longer than a heartbeat. I will
die. I hide in the night
sky, keep you awake; my
pale face, that probing
moon sense, my fingers
of white light on the sheets.

Sunday Morning, Chai Ritual

Bare feet pale on the ash
wood floor, a breeze
through the open window,
outside, cedar fronds loop
and rustle.

A handful of anise,
cloves, two per cup,
pods of cardamom
cracked with the teeth
to free the black seeds,
cinnamon sticks broken
in half, one bay leaf,
black tea.

Simmer. Add milk.
Leave it to bubble
a little, along
the pot's edges.

I teach him this.
He does this
for me.

And Then I Leave You and Piazzola on the Dance Floor

Crows extrapolate,
smart as apes: lines of beaks, telephone

wires, minor keys. We struggle
silently, the metronome

takes over, minutes tick, the tango
breathes a chord, a rib, a cheek, a wrong.

I flick the black wings of my skirt,
crowd the bandoneon,

staccato eighths, your silk shirt sweat-stained,
the violin's pizzicato, long

legs,
      click of silver heels.

The Ribs of the House

A crow and I argued over an apple
before I left for Seville. Now
the grey tree, unpruned, stands
in a fall of yellow apples, one or two
like ornaments on each branch.

The wet road blackens the dog's white paws.
A winter vineyard is a glimmer
of wire lines, and a just-absent sun
feathers the under-wings of clouds spread
over the December valley. I hug
my red shawl around me.

My dog is back
to her old self. She's lost weight.
I see the patch on her side has healed
where she pulled out her fur, chewed
her own flesh, the week you punched
a hole through the wall
of the hallway. We were outside
the spare bedroom. You glared at me
as if to say it was all my fault.

It's been two months
and you finally patched things up
for Christmas. Ridges of plaster stain
the wall: the white not true
to the original, grey
around the edges.

Absence

At this time of day, it's neither
dark nor light. Nobody waits for us
at the top of the driveway.
It's just you and me. Rain
drips off the south side of the roof
as we approach the house.
Blackened daisy heads incline
toward a narrow Japanese maple
losing its leaves. Natural
selection has sheared delphinium,
stargazer lily, columbine. Lavender
has two years of bracts, the older
ones more compact, grey.
This garden has outgrown the deer.
The house has been empty
of you and me, the children
we were going to have, all
our good intentions. We built
the addition from the fir and cedar
that we cut on the property
to make room. Now I am
tired. Under the rake
of the roof, a window is open.
When we enter the front
door, a finch starts to flap
wildly around the kitchen – her nest
is under the eaves – I run
to the window, open it wide
and she flies out.

The Circle, the Dance

The chandelier, high ceilings, wide
boards of the floor: this
is old Berlin. She has entered
from a June night, her head foggy

from jet lag, the train ride, all
the new men. He walks toward her
with confident eyes, hands
that know tango. Something

she doesn't remember until
later. He speaks to her in English.
Biagi plays. Or Tanturi. A playful
bandoneon, strings: experienced

old tangos. He takes her hand
to bring her into the circle, the dance,
the dancers. He takes her
into his body. To dance is to enter

the beat, the heat of the man,
to feel his thigh against hers,
to gasp as he takes small quick
steps; walks into her.

The music ends
and it is the German way
to hold on, so she lets him hold her,
feels his stillness before she steps away.

The Woman Who Teaches Tango

Men confuse me. When the man at the table near the door puts his drink down, walks over and asks me to dance, I expect anything. He might mean, *You're a woman. I'm a man. Neither of us is wearing a wedding ring. Do you want to come home with me?*

I notice the sound his shoes make on the floor, his heels clicking together to accentuate the beat. If I were to have sex with someone tonight it would not be this man with the neat black shirt, hip hair, Dolce & Gabbana cologne. 'Masculine.' I recognize the scent.

I place my left hand along the line of his deltoid muscle, take his left hand with the fingertips of my right, and hold him firmly away from me like a soiled shirt. He spins me around himself, pulling me slightly off balance on each step. Feeling the firmness of my "embrace," how I hold the space between us, he is encouraged to try a complicated step. Then catches my eye and grins. I look away.

The fancy stuff doesn't impress me. The first thing is to learn how to walk, I want to tell him. But now it seems I've forgotten how to dance, feel confused about which foot goes next, lean up against him when I lose my balance. All the men in the dance hall are looking at me. I look down at the scuffed oak floor, the black streaks on it, from peoples' shoes.

About You

I write a poem to argue
with all your maps, the preciseness
of streets, their implied numbers.
The poem suggests doorways, nesting
courtyards; stretches underneath the curve
of f(x) equals 3x squared plus 4x plus 7.
The poem is lean and ragged
around the edges, a little
thin in the middle;
questions all your answers, surprises
you, as the June scent of Unter den Linden,
Tai Chi by the Brandenburg Gate,
a discouraged angel, holding
the wind in your arms.

Here and There

A whole genus of mushrooms covers my driveway when I return home:
Shaggy Manes droop in mournful clusters at the road; tiny yellow fungi
hide halfway up, bright as my dog's eyes; near the top, a mushroom
shaped like a table, where racoons gathered while I was away, to
celebrate the September rains, unguarded garbage can.

Nobody has removed the azaleas burned from summer drought.
The crocosmia is crowded with two seasons of leaves, dead just from
living. A gardener told me it is impossible to eradicate: root bulbs stack
up year after year like apartments.

Like the apartment I just left in Berlin, without plant boxes on its
balconies: your flat, in a building that survived the WW II bombs, you,
who dance at night, sleep in, miss meals.

Nobody I met there could tell me the names of the trees in the
courtyard, not even in German, but we enjoyed their leafy shade as we
sat at sidewalk cafés, drank latté macchiato, *wiessbier*, debated the
architectural features of the Palace Der Republik, a stern asbestos-lined
symbol of old East Germany.

You kissed me on the lips at the end of a dance, we cycled home.
A cool mist settled over the Tiergarten.

Silver

As I lie curled on my side
on sunny morning sheets, aware
of my underwear twined
around my ankle, I feel as
flexible as the gold wire a jeweler
forms into a ring; complete
as the circle it makes.

Was it June, the first time
jumping into the lake with you?
The water touched me all over,
awakened the little hairs on my skin,
cooled my inner thighs.

We floated, watched a bird
with a tuft of feathers on his head
disappear underwater, bring a fish to his mate
and fledglings, swimming in circles by the reeds.

I remember your winter skin, narrow hips
as you walked out of the water,
my own quick steps to the sand,
bathing suit damp and heavy;
how you roughed me up with a towel,
laughed at my bird's-nest hair.

Winter approaches, you are far away,
I am alone in the sunshine.
The yellow leaves outside tremble
and beckon. I turn the heavy silver
ring on my third finger.

Longing

It isn't what you think it will be.

It keeps you up in the night,
competes with birdsong
to wake you at dawn.

She asks if I have it,
as though I am pregnant, or know
I am about to die.

Make it a friend, the therapist tells me. *Don't resist,
or judge, don't give it any power*.

It rolls me gently onto my stomach,
with a sudden jerk pulls down on my leg.

I yell with the surprise of it.

It dives at me, confused by my red T-shirt, then
flies to the top of the tallest fir tree.
All I see – its orange throat,
a beacon.

It rubs against itself, the sound
of two trees, close together,
the creak and whine.

It is a cloak I pull on around myself.
As I stride the long hallway,
the lining flares red.

Stealing From the World

I.

you say
the world is a long glass
of water

thirsty soul

II.

our first evening   a tango
I sit with another man   find
your eyes

III.

you lead another
night with your fingers
on the piano   you summon
strings sing me
verses of James Joyce   your golden hair
chamber music
for a woman walking
behind herself

IV.

The winds are breathing low . . .

V.

I don't know
where I'm going to let you
follow me

we take a few steps   *caminar*

VI.

two curly heads
on a pillow one dark one
bright   long bodies

morning runs light fingers
up and down

VII.

a container

a single note
repeated

The Travelers

Goodnight, good luck, a merry Christmas, and God bless all of you, all of you on the good earth.

- Frank Borman, Commander, Apollo 8, radio message

They found it
surprising, he said, after
coming all this way, what enchanted
them most, what held
their minds from trajectory
corrections and flight plans, error
margins or winning a space
race, was looking back
at the blue earth.

The rocket engine
ignited briefly, their craft dropped
into the gravity well, free
falling on the far
side of the moon, out
of radio contact
with mission control.
Over the moon's
horizon, Earth rose
as if for the first time.

The Space Station Passes Over Salt Spring Island

Krikalev looks out the window into space.
A moonless night approaches: Earth is mostly sea.
He slips into a sleeping bag clipped to the wall
of the station; he floats asleep.

Below, on Salt Spring Island, the blueberry man pours
berries into green cardboard containers. Heather fires the oven
for fruit breads. In the dying light, Stowell Creek farmers
collect summer squash, green beans, arugula. At Moonstruck,
cheeses are wrapped and named *Blossom's Blue,*
White Grace, Blue Moon.

You and I, just home from our honeymoon,
walk down a rutted road at dusk, holding hands,
catch a flash of reflected light
passing overhead, in the southwestern sky.

In The Poem

I won't tell you
about how morning stretches
under the clouds on English Bay
like a bright skin, how
its edges blur tenderly into
the dark, how all moments
accordion into this one
where we touch a stranger's
fingers, how our steps echo
in the street, how you measure
this, the Pont Neuf, my stride,
how you read my back
with your hand, how my sidelong
thoughts slip by
the Seine, out of streets
of the Marais, sniff around you,
intercept a glance, a sudden
kiss before the inevitable
commutation, the door closing
and the gleaming train.

Offering to the Awakened Spirit

Every year on Mansell Road, among dead
blackberry vines and salal,
by the ditch, beside the barbed wire
fence, a pink trillium blooms.

Winter Day, Texas Coast

The sea glimmers after a season of hurricanes.
A cardinal lands just out of sight in the dry trees;

a spoonbill's wings flash pink in the long sun
as it strides through the salt marsh looking

for fish, and then swings its spatulate beak in a wide
arc, back and forth, as it wades on narrow legs, a sharp

turn, back and forth, through course and lapse of tide.
On their southern point of migration, three

whooping cranes rustle their wide wings,
pluck Port Aransas blue crabs

from the marsh grass; the horizon darkens
with flight: a formation of double-crested cormorants.

A pelican drops like a sudden happiness, pops up
in the water, rearranges its wings. A snowy egret

crosses the inlet, pauses, strikes. It is the end
of a long passage, and the beginning.

Notes

The following poems, ("Moose Factory, Ontario;" "The Girl From Attawapiskat;" "First Pregnancy;" "Death Certificate;" "Dear God") contain sections which are based on 18 years of practicing rural and emergency medicine in several small and medium-sized communities. I discuss many situations and events common to a physician practicing in this setting, and the patients in the stories are composites created from my overall clinical experience, and my clinical reading; they do not represent real persons.

p. 13 "A Scent of Cloves"
Richard Francis Burton, 1821 – 1890, was a writer, translator of the Kama Sutra, and an explorer of Zanzibar and East Africa.

p. 22 "Solo"
Beryl Markham was the first person to fly west across the Atlantic, solo, which she did in 1936. This was the more difficult direction to cross because of the strong prevailing winds.

p. 29 "Vocabulary: A Tango"
Abrazo, vals, caminata, ocho, volcada, gancho, molinete, sacada, parada, salida, cruz, el sanguchito, colgada, voleo, cambio de frente are Spanish words which describe movements of Argentine Tango.

p. 45 "La Cumparsita"
La Cumparsita is traditionally the last tango played at a milonga (tango dance).

p. 53 "Dry Tears of a Man"
On the prairies, people trained their dogs to eat only from the owner's hand because of the risk of them eating poison set out for gophers.

p. 60 "The Invisible Buddha"
Quotation from environmentalist David Brower: *We do not inherit the earth from our ancestors; we borrow it from our children.*

p. 63 "My Only Real Virginity"
The title is part of a line taken from "Letter to an Old Lover" by Gwendolyn MacEwan. *"It was you who claimed my only real virginity . . ."*

p. 77 "Stealing From the World"
The italicized line is from "Chamber Music" by James Joyce.

Acknowledgements

Grateful acknowledgement is made to the following magazines and anthologies in which some of the poems were first published, often in different forms: *Arc, Descant, Event, Prism International*, and *Room of One's Own; Dinner Party* and *Letters We Never Sent* by Leaf Press; *Tempus* by Rubicon Press; and *Coming Home* by Rainbow Publishers. The poems "In the Poem" and "Longing" were shortlisted for *Arc's* "Poem of the Year" competitions in 2005 and 2006, also in somewhat different forms.

The author wishes to thank the Banff Centre for funding.

Finally, I wish to thank my community of poets – including Robert Gore, the Waywords (Andrea, Cynthia, Grace, Pamela and Yvonne) and my Salt Spring poetry group (Chris, Diana, Jane, Murray and Shirley) – for years of invaluable feedback and encouragement; and Lorna Crozier and Patrick Lane. Special thanks go to Robert Hilles, Phyllis Webb, and Elizabeth Philips.

The proceeds of this book will be donated to the Vancouver Foundation, and directed toward programs for Aboriginal youth, and for suicide prevention.

About the Author

PHOTO BY ERIC LANOIX

Karen Shklanka is a poet, a family physician and, with her husband, an Argentine Tango dance instructor. Her work was included in the 2004 chapbook anthology, *Letters We Never Sent*, edited by Patrick Lane. She was a finalist for *Arc* magazine's international poem contest in 2005 and 2006, and has been published in many other literary periodicals. *Sumac's Red Arms* is her first book publication.

Born in Toronto, Karen Shklanka spent 15 years practicing rural and emergency medicine in small and medium-sized Canadian communities, and has lived in Sydney, Australia, Houston, Texas, Vancouver, Regina, Moose Factory, Salt Spring Island and Los Angeles at various times in her life. She currently lives in Vancouver, where she serves as a Clinical Instructor in the Faculty of Family Medicine at UBC.